Little B
WOODEN BOXES

WOODEN BOXES CREATED BY THE MASTERS

Little Book of
WOODEN BOXES

WOODEN BOXES CREATED BY THE MASTERS

Peter Korn, Curator

Little Book of Wooden Boxes contains content from *New Masters of the Wooden Box*, first published in 2009 by Fox Chapel Publishing Company, Inc.

ISBN 978-1-56523-996-8

The Cataloging-in-Publication Data is on file with the Library of Congress.

To learn more about the other great books from Fox Chapel Publishing, or to find a retailer near you, call toll-free 800-457-9112 or visit us at *www.FoxChapelPublishing.com*.

We are always looking for talented authors. To submit an idea, please send a brief inquiry to acquisitions@foxchapelpublishing.com.

Printed in Singapore
First printing

CONTENTS

INTRODUCTION
by Oscar Fitzgerald

Boxes are among the most ancient of humankind's works. Usually with four sides, a bottom, and a lid, boxes contain everything imaginable. Lids can be either hinged to the case or detachable, and secured with a hasp or lock to protect the contents. They can be as large as a big-box store or small enough to hold cufflinks.

Ancient Boxes

The numerous boxes recovered from King Tutankhamen's tomb were typical of those that held everyday items the pharaohs would need in the afterlife. One small box held the mummified bodies of two stillborn babies that may have been the king's children. A rectangular wooden box with a hunchbacked lid was decorated with scenes of the hunt or of battles painted on ivory panels on the top, and with floral and animal depictions on the sides. It probably held the king's robes. Like most of the wooden boxes found in the tomb, it was made with mortise-and-tenon joints and carefully cut dovetails—the same joints used by woodworkers today. The box was secured by string threaded around mushroom-shaped knobs and tied with a knot that was then sealed.

After the fall of the Roman Empire, boxes survived in monasteries and castles in Europe during the Middle Ages.

Box with angels, intended to contain small bottles of holy oils. Champlevé enamel over gilt copper, early thirteenth century, Limoges (Limousin, France).

Many held vestments, holy relics, incense, and plate. Small caskets or decorated boxes served as jewel or valuables boxes. Larger cast-iron boxes were common, and medieval dispatch boxes typically had two keys, one each for sender and recipient.

Work Boxes

By the seventeenth century, a box maker's guild had been incorporated in England, and its members specialized in wooden boxes with compartments and drawers and slanting lids to hold books for reading. Serving as the portable desks of the time, these boxes held valuable books, writing equipment, and papers. In the eighteenth century, as papers and accounts proliferated and boxes grew larger, they were placed on stands, and the modern desk was born.

Both men and women used dressing boxes in the seventeenth and eighteenth centuries. Ones for men contained razors, strops and hones, scissors, penknives, and a looking glass. In his *The Cabinet-Maker and Upholsterer's Drawing-Book* (1792), Thomas Sheraton illustrated a square "Lady's Traveling Box" fitted up for writing, dressing, and sewing equipment. It contained compartments for ink and an adjustable writing surface covered with green cloth; a place for scissors and powder, pomatum, and perfume bottles; and a removable dressing glass. There was even a space to store rings and a clever little windlass for rolling up lace as it was worked.

Snuff and Tobacco Boxes

The heyday for English boxes was in the eighteenth century, and often the most extravagant work was lavished on the tiny snuffbox. After the discovery of tobacco in the New World in the seventeenth century, the elaborate ritual of inhaling powdered tobacco spread throughout Europe. Many gentlemen owned multiple boxes to match their various degrees of dress and the formality of the occasion. Madame de Pompadour, mistress of Louis XV, reputedly had a different snuffbox for every day of the year.

Unusual English wooden snuffbox fitted with a carved mechanical snake that strikes when the lid is slid open.

By the nineteenth century, the custom of taking snuff declined, and cigarette and cigar smoking increased. As elegant snuffboxes fell out of fashion, they were replaced with larger cigarette and cigar cases. Wooden boxes were inexpensive to make, and by the late-nineteenth century the familiar, six-board cigar box was common. Cigarette and cigar boxes survived well into the twentieth century, though they were mostly of cardboard.

Gift and Souvenir Boxes

As a measure of their preciousness, snuffboxes were often given as gifts or to celebrate heroic deeds or special events. Boxes were issued to commemorate the hot-air balloon assent of the Montgolfier brothers in the late-eighteenth century and to celebrate the victory of Admiral Vernon over the Spanish at Portobello in 1739.

Sailors who made scrimshaw ditty boxes and other items for their loved ones at home continued the tradition of gift boxes into the nineteenth century. In Germany, and also in Pennsylvania, where so many of their countrymen immigrated during the eighteenth century, brides would be given painted oval or round boxes decorated with flowers and figures as a traditional wedding present containing trinkets and ribbons.

Boxing Day, falling the day after Christmas, is celebrated in Britain, Canada, and several other countries, as a day to give gift boxes to servants and tradespeople. Although the exact origin of the custom is obscure, it may relate to the practice of opening church poor-boxes at Christmas time, or to the fact that servants had to work on Christmas Day and were rewarded the day after with gifts—much like today's Christmas bonus.

Personal Boxes

In addition to gift boxes, a number of other specialized containers were popular in the eighteenth and nineteenth centuries. Gentlemen carried nutmeg and graters to flavor their custard, and had pillboxes in their pockets. Different boxes held breath mints and candy, often in elegant boot-shaped boxes and other forms.

Comfit boxes filled with candied fruit or seeds were also popular during the nineteenth century.

Women carried round, oval or heart-shaped patch boxes to store swatches of silk or taffeta that they applied to their faces to hide the ravages of smallpox and other blemishes. Fancy boxes of silver, gold, ivory, or enamel were often fitted with a gum-pot and brush to stick the fabric patch to the cheek. Other boxes, similar to women's compacts today, held mirrors, rouge, and kohl for the eyes.

Among the ubiquitous containers are jewelry boxes, usually fitted with satin

or velvet and divided into compartments to hold expensive body adornments.

This early nineteenth century, curly maple, schoolgirl box was probably made at the Bath, Maine, Female Academy. It is painted with romantic, ancient Greek and Roman scenes, including the eruption of Mount Vesuvius in 79 C.E.

By the mid-eighteenth century, trinket boxes to hold less-expensive items became popular. Trinkets were essentially small ornaments including jewelry, but also chains, beads, buckles, ribbons, and pendants. The women at female academies that sprung up around the United States in the early nineteenth century decorated many of these square or octagonal boxes. Trinket boxes and jewelry boxes continue in popularity to this day.

Boxes for Clothes

Most clothing was folded and stored in boxes or chests, not hung in closets, until well into the nineteenth century. Hats required their own special boxes. Since the seventeenth century, special boxes protected hats fashioned of costly beaver pelts. Tricorn hats made of felt required

Descendent of the nineteenth century bandbox, this container with the E. Stone store label of New York City once contained women's fancy dress accoutrements from the early twentieth century.

triangular boxes usually of cardboard lined with newspaper. By the early nineteenth century, the tricorn was superseded by felt top hats with high crowns and narrow brims. The height of the crown and the width of the brim varied from year to year, much like the width of modern-day ties. Women, who seldom went bare-headed in the eighteenth or nineteenth centuries, stored their bonnets in special boxes too, along with their stylish ivory, horn, or tortoiseshell combs.

Although some of the cardboard boxes came with cotton bags to protect them, the most durable boxes were fabricated out of wood. Used mostly as trunks during travel, bandboxes fell out of favor as trains and steamboats replaced coach travel. For that, durable, leather-covered, wooden trunks decorated with brass tacks were necessary.

Boxes in the Kitchen

With the introduction of tea drinking into England by Catherine of Braganza, the Portuguese wife of Charles II in the seventeenth century, tea caddies proliferated. (A "caddy" was originally a measure of weight, but it soon became associated with the container for tea.) Usually with two compartments, these little boxes held both black and green tea.

Since colonial times, salt was used primarily as a preservative, but also for seasoning. Saltboxes with slanted lids typically hung on the wall near the hearth to keep the salt dry. Most were wood and, at least in Pennsylvania, were usually painted with tulips, floral decorations, or geometric motifs.

Before the days of glass jars and tin cans, the pantry was filled with numerous round or oval boxes up to two feet in diameter mostly purchased from local woodworkers.

Rectangular ones, often on a stand, held bread dough. Large ones held butter, cheese, and herbs. Smaller ones contained sugar and meal. The smallest were for spices.

Mid-nineteenth century yellow pine wall box from Virginia's Shenandoah Valley constructed with pegs joining the sides and the bottom in the German tradition. These boxes were usually hung by the fire to keep the salt that was often stored in them dry.

The Shakers made the best ones. They steam-bent ash or maple strips around molds, secured the strips with copper rivets, added pine bottoms and tops, and then painted or varnished the entire assembly. As with wooden desk boxes, the wooden storage container gradually lost out to the tin boxes that proliferated after 1800.

North American Indian Boxes

After their exposure to Europeans in the mid-eighteenth century, the Eskimos or Inuit Indians in Alaska used ivory from prehistoric mammoths or walrus tusks to fashion small boxes for needles and snuff. Because of the absence of trees in the Arctic, wooden boxes were rare but a few driftwood boxes for tools, sewing supplies, and tobacco have survived. Like the ivory ones, they were often carved in the shape of a seal or walrus.

The Haida, Tlingit, Tsimshian, and Kwakiutl Indians living along the Northwest Coast of North America produced quite different boxes. Many of them were made for the feasting and exchange of gifts that characterized their great potlatch ceremonies. The best boxes were constructed of cedar, decorated with incised carving, inlaid with abalone shell, and then painted. The boxes were made of a single plank with three kerfs cut into the board so that it could be steam-bent into the shape of a rectangular box and then either fastened together at the open corner with pegs or laced up with cedar roots. Smaller boxes were made of ivory and carved with stylized bear, owl, raven, and killer whale images, all of which played a part in their cultural mythology.

Into the 20th Century

By the twentieth century, handmade boxes fell out of favor as large factories met the demand for containers. Food was now stored in glass bottles, plastic jars, or cardboard boxes. If we want to store something, it is usually in a cardboard box or a plastic container. We write at desk computers or laptops, not elegant wooden lap desks.

As bathrooms became an essential component of twentieth century homes, dressing boxes largely disappeared as most men and women stored their body care products in wall cabinets or on the sink counter.

With the exception of decorative boxes for special uses, most modern boxes are made of solid or woven plastic, cardboard, or tin, and are designed for specific utilitarian purposes. Document boxes still exist, but they take the form of plastic boxes, metal-filing cases, or simple cardboard boxes with no tops. Plastic organizers provide specialized compartments for the detritus that clutters the modern desk.

In some quarters, jewelry boxes have morphed into something entirely unexpected. When compact discs became popular in the early 1980s, the Polygram record division of Philips Electric designed a thin, plastic box to hold them based loosely on the familiar plastic audiocassette box developed in the 1960s. They soon became known as jewel cases, not because they held anything rare—in 1990 alone, nearly 300 million were made—but because the hinge on the case worked like the arbors in watches that spin on tiny jewels.

The box-making tradition survives today, if largely as an art form. Since World War II and the resurgence of handcraftsmanship, the interest in fine boxes has grown. In the eighteenth and nineteenth centuries many boxes were turned out of both wood and metal, but by and large they were utilitarian and plain. Today, however, turning has evolved into a high art, and turned boxes are among the most creative containers. The tradition of fine wooden boxes as luxury items was not revived until the second half of the twentieth century.

Most traditional turned boxes took the form of simple cylinders. Lids were added to vase-shaped vessels. It was an easy leap to add a turned top to a turned vase-shaped vessel, making it into a box. Common in the nineteenth century, these turned boxes were more ornamental than useful, but they were still boxes.

Over the centuries, the box has evolved into many specialized forms to hold every conceivable object. Today, objects and their containers overwhelm us and we even rent off-site storage in which to hold them. However, the handcrafted boxes in this book are in another category. They are the result of countless hours of highly skilled labor, creative talent, and imagination. In the process, the makers have left their unique fingerprints and a bit of their soul in their boxes.

These artists speak with their hands and we are inspired to listen.

–Oscar P. Fitzgerald

BONNIE BISHOFF and J.M. SYRON

Bonnie Bishoff and J.M. Syron met on Martha's Vineyard in 1987, she fresh out of college and he taking a break from furniture making in Boston. They have been collaborating as artists ever since. He does most of the construction for their pieces, and she does the fine carving and polymer clay designs. Her inspirations are nature, Native American carving, and Art Nouveau.

b. 1963 Philadelphia, Pennsylvania (Bonnie); 1960 Columbus, Ohio (J.M.)

Background: Bonnie: Woodblock printing and theater set construction at Oberlin College; grandfather was tool-and-die maker; mother was tailor. **J.M.** Studied tool-and-die making at Westchester Community College and trained in furniture making; mother was fiber artist.

Studio location: Brunswick, Maine

www.syronbishoff.com

Our work is a lot about melding things, partly because we're collaborating, but we're also bringing two mediums together.

—Bonnie Bishoff

Inner Eye Box, 2008. Bird's-eye maple, basswood, polymer clay; H. 9" W. 18" D. 9".

Pumpkin Box, 2004. Mahogany, polymer clay; H. 7"
Dia. 7". Summer and winter squash served as a model
for *Pumpkin Box*, their first box made by molding
polymer clay around a form.

BONNIE BISHOFF AND J.M. SYRON

Above left: **Sun and Shade Wall Hung Cabinet,** 2006. Walnut, polymer clay; H. 26" W. 20" D. 12". Essentially a functional painting, *Sun and Shade Wall Hung Cabinet* was inspired by antique Japanese theater kimonos with botanical patterns and color blocks.

Above: *Winter Woods Coffer,* 2006. Walnut, cherry, polymer clay; H. 18" W. 22" D. 16". Winter walks in the snow are always an inspiration. *Winter Woods Coffer* was constructed during a howling winter blizzard.

Persian Box, 2004. Cherry, polymer clay; H. 6" W. 8" D. 8". Named after the domed roofs of ancient Persia, *Persian Box* was an early attempt at something small, functional, collectable, and unique in its use of polymer clay.

BONNIE BISHOFF AND J.M. SYRON

Inner Eye Box, 2008. Bird's-eye maple, basswood, polymer clay; H. 9" W. 18" D. 9".

Woodland Shade Vessel, 2004. Walnut, polymer clay; H. 11" W. 17" D. 10". *Woodland Shade Vessel* relates to the Islesboro series, and the pattern in the clay body grew out of an interest in ornamental hostas.

BONNIE BISHOFF AND J.M. SYRON

Sea and Sky Altar Coffer, 2006. Mahogany, polymer clay; H. 26" W. 27" D. 19". Based on a ceremonial coffer, *Sea and Sky Altar Coffer* was made for the 2007 Inspired by China exhibit. It holds Lakota Indian prayer ties that Bishoff used in a healing ceremony after spinal surgery. The "cracked ice" latticework and the wave and cloud forms on the exterior are traditional Chinese motifs.

Java Credenza, 2002. Mahogany, pommele sapeli, polymer clay; H. 38" W. 56" D. 24". *Java Credenza* was the couple's first attempt at creating a large case piece using polymer clay veneers. The piece recalls French Art Deco furniture.

BONNIE BISHOFF AND J.M. SYRON

ANDY BUCK

 Although principally a furniture maker, he has produced many boxes during his career and thinks of his cabinets as just big boxes. Buck's muted color palette is influenced by artist Paul Klee, who believed color could touch the spirit in the same way music does. Buck hopes his furniture will transform an interior space the way music changes the mood of an environment.

He likes his projects to wear that patina of wear and age. Weathered finishes and folk references recall the handmade objects his father brought back from trips to Africa, Indonesia, and New Guinea while working for the World Health Organization. He is a full professor at Rochester Institute of Technology, where he teaches woodworking and industrial design.

b. 1966 Baltimore, Maryland

Background: Andy stumbled into woodworking when he needed art credits while studying political science at Virginia Commonwealth University; holds an MFA in industrial design/furniture from Rhode Island School of Design.

Studio location: Honeoye Falls, New York

andybuck.com

Mr. Red, 2008. Mahogany, ebony; H. 20" W. 20" D. 6".

Black and White with Broom, 1993. Ash, copper, bristle; H. 69" W. 21" D. 12". The writings of Joseph Campbell on the power of myth inspired this cabinet. Examining the ritual of cleaning, Buck deifies the common broom.

Decoys, 2003. Walnut, mahogany,
poplar; H. 21" W. 14" D. 9". Two of
a series of twenty-seven birds Buck
carved for an exhibition.

KIP CHRISTENSEN

Kip Christensen is a versatile turner best known for his lidded containers. His interest in boxes stems from exposure to the work of the turner and box maker Del Stubbs, who attended the Utah Woodturning Symposiums that Kip helped organize in the late 1970s and early 1980s. Christensen was impressed with how challenging making a box could be. Obviously, the lid needs to fit, but should it fit loosely and come off easily? Fit tightly and open with a crisp popping sound? Or something in between?

He likes to create objects that are more tactile than functional, and correspondingly he spends the most time on surface finish rather than the object itself. He subjects his surfaces to a series of controlled abuses such as sandblasting, bleaching, and sanding to achieve a complex, mottled effect. Recognized as the first craftsman to turn boxes from elk antlers, Kip uses a laborious process to counteract the porous nature of the centers of antlers. After turning the antler for a while, he applies cyanoacrylate glue to fill the pores and then turns some more—repeating the process several times.

b. 1955 Preston, Indiana

Background: Grew up working in family-owned cabinet factory; earned bachelor's and master's degrees in industrial education from Brigham Young University, where he now serves on the Ira A. Fulton School of Engineering and Technology faculty.

Studio location: Provo, Utah

Form comes first. There seems to be no other quality that has the power to compensate for poor form.

Whited Sepulchre, 2004. Russian olive burl; H. 5" Dia. 6". This series was born after a family trip to Bryce Canyon, Utah, where Christensen was inspired by the natural texture of the land. Portions of the surface have been sanded, sandblasted, and bleached.

Lidded Box, 1995. Macassar ebony; H. 1¾" Dia. 3". Form is paramount. In Lidded Box, the shape of the body echoes the shape of the lid, which in turn is shaped for ease of removal. Note how the light sapwood on the base is perfectly proportioned with the sapwood exposed on the lid.

Box, 1997. Blackwood, moose antler, turquoise; H. 2¾" Dia. 1¾". This box invites handling and close inspection. It required precision turning and flawless finishing.

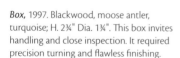

Small Vessel and Bowl, 1997. Blackwood, turquoise; H. ¾" Dia. 3". The two pieces are linked in form as well as materials. Blackwood and turquoise are among Christensen's favorite materials.

Miscellaneous Antler Pieces, 1997. Elk antler, ebony, pink ivory wood; H. 2½" Dia. ¾". Christensen's first antler series began as simple shallow bowls. A natural edge came next, followed by a contrasting ring of blackwood or pink ivory wood embellished with small turquoise beads.

Antler Box, 2007. Elk antler, turquoise,
African blackwood; H. 2½" Dia. 3½".

KIP CHRISTENSEN

Inlaid Box, 2003. Box elder burl, blackwood; H. 3" Dia. 4½". *Inlaid Box* features a delicate ring of blackwood highlighting the figure in the box elder burl. The simplicity of the design belies the steps necessary to ensure dimensional stability. The wood is roughed out, dried, re-roughed out, and dried again to ensure it is stable.

Tower Box, 2007. Box elder burl, blackwood, amboyna burl; H. 7" Dia. 2¾".

JIM CHRISTIANSEN

Jim Christiansen finds bugs beautiful and complex. How do they move all those joints in their legs? he asks. How do they find their way? With such tiny brains, how do they learn the skills of their trade? What are they thinking? This universal, or near universal, fascination with bugs is part of the appeal of Christiansen's work.

In addition to his bugs, his fossil vessels evolved from a childhood curiosity about dinosaurs. The wood grain reminded him of soil under which dinosaur bones could possibly be buried. That led to inlaying carved bones on his turned vessels to suggest fossils. Like his bug boxes, the fossils are not exact copies but rather artistic suggestions.

b. 1943 Ogden, Utah

Background: Served in the US Air Force; earned degrees in special education from University of Utah and Utah State and ultimately left career in school administration to pursue woodturning full time.

Studio location: Moscow, Idaho

Bob, 2008. Curly maple, ebony, wengé, brass; H. 12" W. 17" D. 10". The idea for *Bob,* Christiansen's fourth bug box, came from the wreckage of a bowl that blew up on his lathe: one of the pieces looked like a scarab beetle. He had read an article about ancient Egyptians' reverence for a dung beetle.

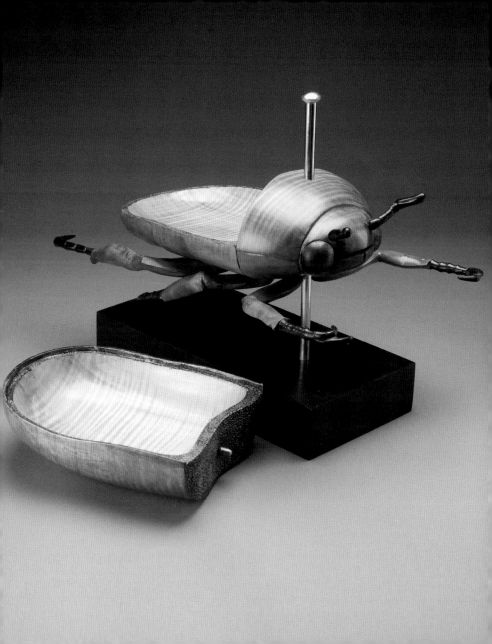

Opposite
Elusive Dreams, 2007. Maple burl, maple; H. 10" Dia. 9". The potential of the good things we visualize inside *Elusive Dreams* is somehow mitigated by the sorrowful figures that support it. Reality tempers our hopes and dreams.

The Offering, 2006. Ribbon mahogany, maple; H. 9" Dia. 15". For Christiansen, the three "bird skull" figures in bondage in *The Offering* represent giving and sacrifice, while the bowl holds things we offer up to others.

Greed, 2005. Maple, maple burl; H. 15" Dia. 10". *Greed* represents Christiansen's strong feelings about unjust war. He turned the box small, so the figures, which he carved separately, would dominate the composition.

Root Box, 1999. Maple burl, ebony; H. 7" Dia. 8". *Root Box,* Christiansen's first carved box, paid homage to the roots that are the ultimate source of the wood.

Root Box, 2008. Mallee burl, walnut, maple; H. 9" Dia. 3½". One of a number of root box variations, *Root Box* combines the formal turned box with an organic root carving.

Archaeopteryx Redux, 2008. Maple burl, eucalyptus burl, walnut; H. 4½" Dia. 8". Adding carved fossil bones, as in *Archaeopteryx Redux*, was an early attempt by Christiansen to decorate his turnings. Over the years, his fossils have gotten much more realistic.

Spider Box, 2008. Ebony, maple, wengé, brass; H. 9" W. 13" D. 13". Christiansen's *Spider Box* was inspired by a ten-year old piece of African ebony. It is not adn exact copy, but rather a sculptural interpretation of the essence of the black widow spider.

JEAN-CHRISTOPHE COURADIN

Jean-Christophe Couradin uses only traditional sculptor's tools—chisels, gouges, rasps, and scrapers—to shape his abstract forms from his favorite types of wood. Those woods include lignum vitae from South America, cocobolo from Mexico, snakewood from Guiana, Macassar ebony, pink ivory from South Africa, rosewood from Brazil, mahogany from Cuba, and boxwood from France.

Inspired by his heroes, the sculptors Constantin Brancusi and Henry Moore, he lets the grain of the wood dictate the form of his sculptures. Consequently, his work has a tactile quality heightened by the contrast between sharp edges and smooth, highly polished curves. Although he thinks of each piece as a sculpture rather than functional object, most of his designs open as boxes with chiseled out drawers that pivot open on pins—a subtle partnership between form and function.

b. 1961 Dijon, France

Background: Began work as furniture carver and cabinetmaker at the age of 18, setting up a cooperative with five friends; father was X-ray machine technician; in 1989 took sculpture classes at Ecole des Beaux-Arts in Grenoble and began to focus exclusively on fine art.

Studio Location: Le Touvet, France

www.sculpture-couradin.com

There is always something that lives under the skin of a piece of sculpture.

Water Sculpture, 2008. Madagascar rosewood; H. 7" W. 12" D. 8½".

JEAN-CHRISTOPHE COURADIN

Passion, 1997. Madagascan rosewood, various inlays; H. 39½" W. 19½" D. 15½". *Passion* was purchased by the town of Grenoble, near where Couradin resides. An example of his "variable geometry," the piece is a smooth interplay of curves until a touch reveals angular parts that peel off to expose exotic inlays.

ANDREW CRAWFORD

A specialist in making jewelry boxes since the mid-1980s, Andrew Crawford prefers rectangle shapes with concave sides and domed lids. The inspiration originally came from a pair of ship's decanters with wide bases that he remembers as a child. He builds his boxes with birch plywood or medium-density fiberboard (MDF) that he shapes with a hollow plane, scrapes, and sands smooth; he joins the sides with blind splines, and fashions the domed lid out of two or three thin strips of birch placed over a form and glued. Drawers open by means of an ingenious pin system that Crawford adapted from similar locking mechanisms on nineteenth century boxes.

It is not the making of boxes per se that Andrew enjoys, but the decorating. The carcass serves as a ground for intricate inlay and veneer. His standard touch is the diamond-shaped escutcheon done in mother-of-pearl or contrasting wood. Finally, he gives each box a French polish.

b. 1955 Dartford, England

Background: Trained as flute player at the Royal College of Music, and performed as rock bass player in London; began woodworking career as instrument repairer in 1986 before specializing in jewelry boxes; great grandfather Tom Rowden was well-known watercolorist.

Studio location: Shropshire, England

www.fine-boxes.com

Lava, 2008. H. 9" W. 16" D. 12". Oak, amboyna veneer, dyed sycamore veneer, ebony, birch plywood.

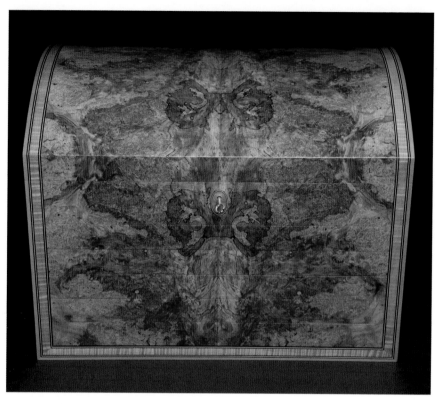

Cufflink Case, 2008. Elm, birch plywood, North American sweet gum burl, figured maple, lemon wood; H. 12" W. 18" D. 12". A single leaf of book-matched elm veneer decorates the front, back, and top of the box.

The maple banding is cut from solid figured maple blanks laminated between black-dyed and maple veneers. Sides and back feature a simple black/white/black band. Square lemonwood strips protect the exterior edges.

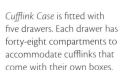

Cufflink Case is fitted with five drawers. Each drawer has forty-eight compartments to accommodate cufflinks that come with their own boxes.

Jewelry Box,
2006. Myrtle,
maple, dyed
veneers;
H. 9" W. 13" D. 5".
The multicolored band
that borders the lid and
front of *Jewelry Box* is made
from dyed veneers. These are
laminated and stacked in the
appropriate order to create a
decorative plank, from which
thin strips are cut. The chest
contains two maple trays lined
with dyed leather.

ANDREW CRAWFORD

MICHAEL CULLEN

A maker of chests, boxes, and tables, Michael Cullen always dreamed of working in a setting surrounded by nature. His shop, in a converted egg sorting plant within bicycling distance from his home, gives him just that. He ornaments the surfaces of his works with nature-inspired carving designs, and his tabletops are covered with rhythmic, geometrical patterns. His tables furthermore reveal his interest in sculpture, beyond the utilitarian mode of making functional furniture. Sometimes, he lines the interior of his chest projects with unfinished redwood burl. The redwood adds the visual and olfactory flavors of his northern California milieu.

His carving technique is a product of a his preference for using a mallet to control his chisel work, which he learned from Maori carver Lynol Grant in New Zealand, and his early appreciation for the works of Judy McKie and Wendell Castle, whose carved furniture and sculptural clocks, respectively, showed him how he could combine his interest in art with his engineering background and make a living as an artist.

b. 1958 Pocatello, Idaho

Background: Michael earned his degree in mechanical engineering from UC Santa Barbara before, in the mid-1980s, pivoting toward furniture making and fine woodworking, gaining experience in Boston's Emily Street workshop coop after completing the Leeds Design Workshop program; both grandfather and great grandfather were cabinetmakers for Southern Pacific Railroad.

Studio location: Petaluma, California

www.michaelcullendesign.com

Elephant Chest, 2000. Mahogany, redwood burl; H. 12" W. 16" D. 10½". The green milk paint captures the green of the grass and oak trees in the Sonoma County mountains near Michael Cullen's home.

Quintet with Cracked Ice (aka Puzzle Tables), 2006.
Mahogany; H. 22" W. 42" D. 42". Made for the 2006
Inspired by China exhibition, these five tables can be
arranged in many different ways. The carved, cracked
ice motif on their tops refracts light in dramatic ways.

MICHAEL CULLEN

Orange Box, 2007. Basswood, ebony;
H. 6" W. 8" D. 2½". *Orange Box,* Cullen's version of a band-sawn box, is
quick to make (in theory) and uses up some perfectly good scrap wood.
This design exhibits the qualities of ceramic vessels that he admires—
curvature, delicateness, and a non-directional quality of the material.

MICHAEL CULLEN

JENNA GOLDBERG

While Jenna Goldberg usually has a general idea of the look she wants, she aims for a gestural, free form quality in her cabinets and boxes. She uses these structures as canvases to display a colorful vocabulary of carved and painted patterns. She attributes her interest in patterns to Islamic art, which she encountered while finishing high school in Israel. She found the abstract mosaics and tiles of mosques and other holy sites mesmerizing, ethereal, and meditative.

Her cabinets and boxes, she says, are like people—different on the inside than on the outside. For instance, she embellishes the insides of some of her pieces with transfer prints from matchboxes popular in the 1940s and 1950s, mostly depicting animals. She photocopies the matchboxes, applies a transfer gel that pulls the ink off the paper, and transfers it onto the wood.

b. 1966 Brewster, New York

Background: Both parents graduated from Rhode Island School of Design and made crafts; earned bachelor's degree in illustration from University of the Arts in Philadelphia and master's degree in furniture design from Rhode Island School of Design.

Studio location: Providence, Rhode Island

www.jennagoldbergstudio.com

Samba Cabinet, 2005. Walnut; H. 75" W. 23" D. 15". The radio was playing Samba music from Brazil when Goldberg was finishing this cabinet. Although walnut is a preferred wood for cabinetry, Goldberg found that it did not provide enough contrast with her paint. The exterior shows off Goldberg's typical abstract geometric forms while the interior is rubber-stamped. The slats in the back are set with gaps between them for air circulation.

Gingko Buffet, 2005. Maple, cherry; H. 38" W. 60" D. 22". The gingko leaves, which she remembers from her time in Philadelphia, are accentuated by freehand carving and give no hint of the surprise that lies inside. Behind the door in the cabinet are blowups of traditional Japanese woodblock prints of landscapes, reproduced from matchboxes.

JENNA GOLDBERG

Bobby H Wall Cabinet, 2004. Basswood; H. 56" W. 22" D. 14". The outside of *Bobby H Wall Cabinet* is an amalgamation of abstract forms from art and design books. The interior features rubber-stamped birds. Goldberg would never want them as pets but likes their shapes and the idea that they are mysterious.

JENNA GOLDBERG

Rose Vanity, 2007. Mahogany; H. 36" W. 72" D. 24". The outside of this vanity is covered with stylized leaves and roses while interior compartments have animals from her Japanese matchbox collection. The drawers are band sawn.

Boxes, 2008. Basswood with Xerox transfers. Blue: H. 4" W. 24" D. 5". Red: H. 4" W. 19" D. 4". Green: H. 4" W. 11" D. 5" .

LOUISE HIBBERT

Louise Hibbert takes inspiration from the ways that nature solves the problems of life and survival. That is why she creates sculptures that show the unusual beauties of nature that are too small or move too fast for most people to appreciate. Throughout her career, she has turned to scientific illustrations from earlier centuries, particularly the work of Ernest Haeckel, whose *Art Forms in Nature* also had an influence on Art Nouveau. And with environmental concerns in mind, she prefers sustainable native British woods, particularly sycamore, whose pale, even grain "when colored glows with an intense vibrancy."

Her long-running collaboration with jeweler Sarah Parker-Eaton has led her to focus on diminutive pieces with an organic appearance. She likes these because people can pick them up, interact with them, and appreciate the exquisite detail. In addition, she can finish them quickly. Best is developing the concept for a new sculpture, and then, fast forwarding, doing the final airbrushing and texturing.

b. 1972 Southampton, England

Background: Grew up by the sea and is motivated by ethic of sustainability; earned degree in three-dimensional design from University of Brighton; uses a 1950 Wadkin Bursgren lathe.

Studio location: Llanfairfechan, Wales

louisehibbert.com

Coleoptera Pill Box, 2009. African blackwood, English sycamore, copper, stainless steel, pine, resin; H. 2¾" W. 5" D. 2". She chose copper to complement the beetle's emerald green body, textured the central section with pyrography, turned the basic shape before carving it, and then airbrushed the elytra (wings) with acrylic inks. A bit of gold dust made the green body iridescent. A fine inlay of patina metal added additional interest.

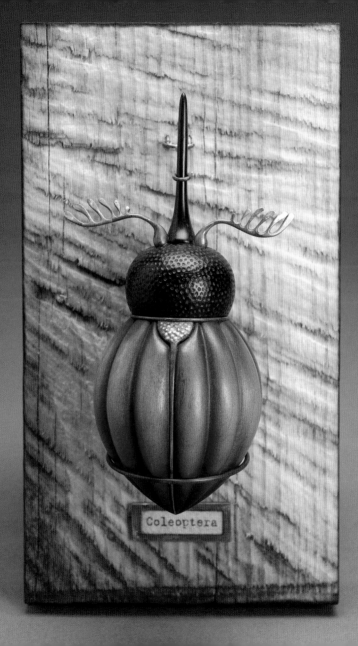

Coleoptera

Lace Bug Box, 2001. English sycamore, silver, African blackwood; L. 4½". The genesis of *Lace Bug Box* came from a glimpse of an image of a delicate lace bug in a museum bookshop. Hibbert made the box during an International Turning Exchange in Philadelphia. Mark Gardner, another artist and craftsman in the program, textured the body. When opened, Lace Bug Box highlights the silver Hibbert experimented with during the International Turning Exchange.

Cinachyra Box, 2000. English sycamore, boxwood, acrylic texture paste, polyester resin; Dia. 4". Typical of her early work, the idea for *Cinachyra Box* started as a golf-ball sponge found in the Western Pacific but represents an amalgamation of many different sea creatures. Hibbert created the interior from an illustration of a radiolarian by Ernst Haeckel.

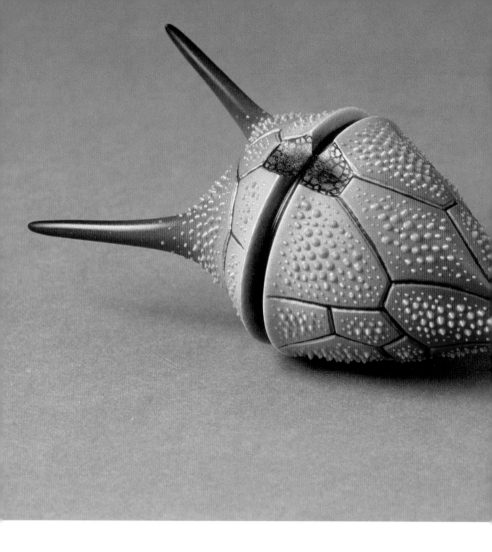

LOUISE HIBBERT

Dinoflagellates Boxes I & II, 2000. I (left): English sycamore, ebony, acrylic ink, polyester resin, acrylic texture paste; L. 10½". II (right): English sycamore, yew, acrylic ink, polyester resin; L. 5". Landscape photographer Tom Carlise commissioned *Dinoflagellates Boxes I & II.* He wanted a plankton-inspired piece that provided both visual and tactile interest, and he specified the colors from a photograph he had taken in Nevada.

Haeckel Pod Box, 2008. English sycamore, silver, maple veneer, reclaimed leather, cotton thread; L. 5½". Before working in wood, Hibbert had focused on textiles. *Haeckel Pod Box,* with a ridged outer casing in leather and a soft lining to protect the inner pod, reminded her of horse chestnuts. Sarah Parker-Eaton fabricated the metal work.

Rhodanthe Box, 2004. English sycamore, silver gold, texture paste; H. 3½". Hibbert picked up a rhodanthe seedpod in Perth, Australia. She wanted to capture its subtle coloring in *Rhodanthe Box.*

LOUISE HIBBERT

MICHAEL HOSALUK

Michael Hosaluk believes his strong grounding in traditional woodworking has given him confidence for projects that are more creative. While still a young woodworker in Canada's Saskatchewan Province, he shifted to creative woodworking and began to exhibit installations in gallery shows. The themes of interaction and relationships came to dominate his oeuvre; he views his sculptural projects as self-expressive art.

What draws him to boxes is their interactive quality. The idea for his *Relationships* series of boxes came from a walk on the beach. The pair of segmented turnings can be moved into any number of configurations to suggest the infinite complexity of human relationships. Opening in the middle, the boxes also can be put back together in different orientations.

b. 1954 Invermay, Canada

Background: Grew up on a farm in Saskatchewan where mother knitted and father made furniture; began cabinetmaking career immediately after high school then shifted to fine art woodworking; helped established world-renowned Emma Lake Collaboration in the 1990s.

Studio location: Saskatoon, Canada

www.michaelhosaluk.com

After a while, self-portraits are evident in all we do.

Relationships, 2005. Australian jara, Canadian maple; H. 7" W. 10" D. 4".

Introvert/Extrovert,
2000. Ash, blackwood;
H. 12" W. 12" D. 5".
These vessels are part
of a series of self-
portraits.

Opposite
Summer Chest, 2002.
Baltic plywood, maple;
H. 36" W. 40" D. 18".
Summer Chest displays
Hosaluk's love of color
and surface pattern.
The decoration was
inspired by Aboriginal
art he had seen in
Australia.

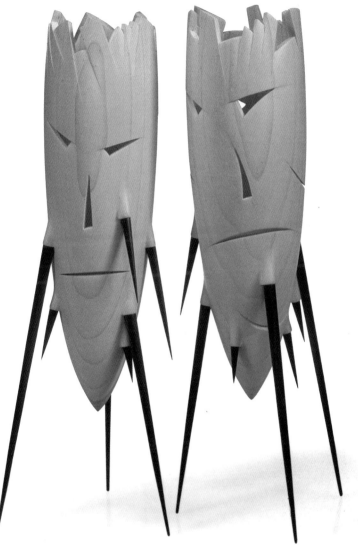

MICHAEL HOSALUK

ROBERT INGHAM

Robert Ingham has always liked containers. His furniture sometimes resembles scaled-up boxes while other times his boxes resemble scaled-down cabinets. His designs are generally restrained, drawing the eye with subtle combinations of light and dark woods. However, a technique he employs frequently involves embellishing with abalone shell, mother-of-pearl, and cut stones to create focal points.

His craftsmanship is impeccable. For example, his drawers are all finely crafted with dovetail and mortise-and-tenon joints. In fact, being obsessed with handcraftsmanship, he eschews any store-bought hardware, preferring to fashion his own wooden joints on machinery he engineered himself.

b. 1938 Delhi, India

Background: Father was officer in colonial police force in India; the family moved to England after Partition; Robert earned teaching degree from Loughborough College and studied design at Leeds College of Art; taught making in school before going into furniture-making business with his brother, which then led to helping establish School for Craftsmen in Wood, Parnham College, where he was principal for 20 years; in private business since 1997.

Studio location: Bwlch Isa, Wales

www.robertinghamdesigns.com

Treasure Chest, 2008. Macassar ebony, Swiss pear, American black walnut, ripple sycamore, abalone shell; H. 7¾" W. 16⅝" D. 9⅜".

*Trio,*1999. Purpleheart, bird's-eye maple; H. 2" W. 5" D. 12". When the lids are lifted, it is hard not to imagine the purpleheart insets as bright red smiling lips.

Lattice Tower, 2004. Silky oak, ripple sycamore with walnut, abalone inlay; H. 48" W. 16" D. 16". The inlaid squares on the front of *Lattice Tower* recall the work of Josef Hoffmann and the Vienna Secessionists of the early twentieth century, while the latticework that forms the feet are a nod to oriental design.

Times 4, 2008. Bog oak, olive ash, walnut, abalone; H. 2" W. 9" D. 9". Discs of abalone highlight each of the four separate lids.

ROBERT INGHAM

Hobson's Choice, 2001. Bird's-eye maple with walnut and abalone inlay; H. 30" W. 48" D. 16". *Hobson's Choice* is the hall table Mr. and Mrs. Hobson commissioned to hold their telephone, with drawers for directories and a cupboard below to house the children's shoes.

RAY JONES

Driven by a love of wood, Ray Jones seeks out salvaged, plantation-grown, or sustainably harvested wood in a variety of species from around the world. Among his favorites are black mangrove, spalted strangler fig, and Indian rosewood. Using no stains or dyes, he finishes the boxes with a mixture of polyurethane, linseed oil, and mineral spirits to produce a silky smooth finish.

Although most turned boxes have lift-off lids, he makes boxes with hinged lids or doors. He likes the interplay of cylinders with curved surfaces; all of the hardware in his boxes is actually wood. He also makes his own plywood by gluing up layers of veneer. By varying the wood species—his go-tos are avodire, mahogany, walnut, and okoume—he produces defect-free plywood in a variety of colors.

b. 1955 Ukiah, California

Background: During college, worked summers for builder who preached self-sufficiency; earned degree in aeronautical engineering from California Polytechnic State University and helped build jet engines for the military, before leaving in the early 1980s to focus on making fine boxes; moved east in 1990 and joined the Southern Highland Craft Guild.

Studio location: Asheville, North Carolina

www.rayjoneswoodboxes.com

Nature has provided a wonderful palette. How can I improve upon that?

Omega V, 2008. Mahogany, pommele bosse, ebony; H. 19" W. 18" D. 8"

Omega V (open), 2008. Mahogany, pommele bosse, ebony; H. 19" W. 18" D. 8"

Production Boxes, 2000. Top to bottom: avodire, spalted beech, chakte kok, mesquite, curly maple, myrtle burl, bird's-eye maple, Cuban mahogany. Smallest: H.1¾" W. 3½" D. 4". Largest: H. 5" W. 15" D. 9". These production boxes have been Jones' staple for more than twenty-six years. Each is made entirely of wood, including the hinges, fasteners, and all hardware. The design is based on a box he made for his future wife in 1981.

Fledgling, 2000. Avodire plywood, madrone burl, ebony; H. 8" Dia. 13". Fledgling is a variation of his Hidden Treasure series. The ebony column in the front is a latch, with a pin that must be raised to open. The other two ebony columns serve as hinges.

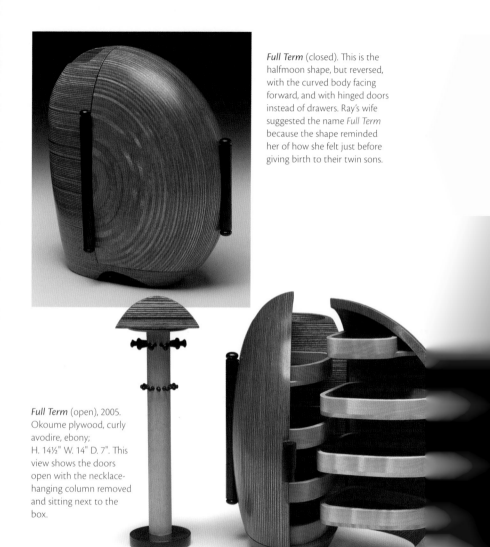

Full Term (closed). This is the halfmoon shape, but reversed, with the curved body facing forward, and with hinged doors instead of drawers. Ray's wife suggested the name *Full Term* because the shape reminded her of how she felt just before giving birth to their twin sons.

Full Term (open), 2005. Okoume plywood, curly avodire, ebony; H. 14½" W. 14" D. 7". This view shows the doors open with the necklace-hanging column removed and sitting next to the box.

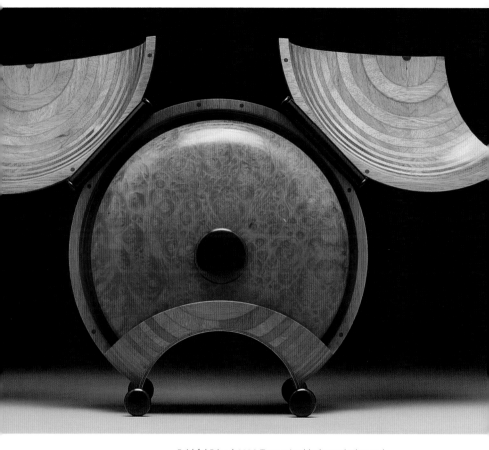

Faithful Friend, 2006. Tasmanian blackwood, plywood, ebony, madrone burl; H. 15" W. 15" D. 8". Designed as a pet cremation urn, the madrone burl vessel, fitted with an ebony stopper on the front, lifts out. A turned pedestal allows *Faithful Friend* to stand with the opening up so that it can be filled.

KIM KELZER

Between big furniture projects, which are her forte, Kim Kelzer likes to make small things like boxes and lamps for change of pace. These projects provide a way to try out new forms, textures, and shapes. For example, she made a series of lamps using parts of 1950s irons that she had been collecting for some time. She embellishes her work with all manner of ornament including mosaics, pottery, and glass, always to make a point, a joke, or both. The surface is often the focal point in her work.

Based on her master's thesis and the example of Judy McKie and other prominent women in the studio furniture movement, she has claimed a style that is characteristically funny, irreverent, and sarcastic; it has marked her as one of the most creative makers in the field.

b. 1957 El Paso, Texas

Background: Took shop classes in high school, father was handy and built an addition to house; earned degree in painting from San Jose State University and master's degree in artisanry from Southeastern Massachusetts University— her thesis was on the influence of pop culture on furniture design; has been making furniture since 1985.

Studio location: Freeland, Washington

Recreational Vehicle Liquor Cabinet, 2001. Wood, glass, found objects, steel; H. 53" W. 14" D. 12". Kelzer created this piece for a show called Recreation/Recreation using recycled materials. Her cabinet revolves around drinking and watching television.

Opposite
Hi/Lo (Red Iron Box), 2005. Huon pine, leather, found metal objects; H. 10" W. 12" D. 4½".

Railroad Cans, 2008. Painted wood; H. 3" to 36". Kelzer's early work used lots of color, texture, and pattern. The pattern is in the variety of the oilcans, and the texture lies in their forms playing off one another.

STEVEN KENNARD

During his time in France, in the 1990s, Steven Kennard became obsessed with styling the surfaces of his projects. Inspired by Canadian turner Stephen Hogbin's work, which showed him how turning could be sculptural by, Steven used watercolor to distinguish his pieces, but eventually moved on to texturing tools—now his signature style.

He uses a Foredom machine, a flexible shaft rotary power tool that can be fitted with different burrs, rasps, and cutters. Also a professional photographer, he will often try to replicate in wood the textures he captures in his photography. He likes to create more figurative boxes—in 1999, creating *Saturn* he realized that a box did not need to have a flat bottom. Many of his boxes involve a turned hollow cone design, precisely weighted to rest upright on any surface.

b. 1956 Enfield, England

Background: Grandfather was a cabinetmaker; began woodworking career designing and building stage sets for British theater group Magic Lantern in the 1970s; began exhibiting in the 1980s before moving first to France in 1989, operating a private studio, then to Nova Scotia Province of Canada in 1997, where he has run his studio since.

Studio location: Canning, Canada

stevenkennard.com

French Connection, 2007. African blackwood, French boxwood; H. 6¼" W. 4" D. 4". Deceptively simple in appearance, this project is in fact the most refined and difficult to make of all the boxes in this series. The Eiffel Tower shape and the French boxwood make the French connection.

Wired, 2005. African blackwood, cocobolo, poplar burl, Plexiglas, mother-of-pearl, steel guitar string; W. 8" Dia. 3". It evokes dreams of a tight ropewalker balancing above the bed.

STEVEN KENNARD

Tread Softly, 2007. African blackwood, cocobolo, French boxwood; H. 2¼" Dia. 3". The surface suggests stone pavers, and the name comes from a W. B. Yeats poem, "I have spread my dreams under your feet. Tread softly because you tread on my dreams." Kennard views his work as spreading his dreams under the feet of those who see it.

Hat in a Box, 2005. Snakewood, African
blackwood; H. 5¼" W. 2½" D. 2½".

STEVEN KENNARD

Birthing Box, 1993. African blackwood, tagua nut; 5" Dia. 3¼". A
metaphor for the creative process, this piece represents pearls moving
from the body up the birth canal to be born at the top and fall down
into the concave base.

YUJI KUBO

Yuji Kobo opened his own lacquer studio in the mid-1980s in his hometown of Hirosaki. The region is home to Tsugaru lacquer, the traditional and most sought-after Japanese lacquer because of its smooth surfaces, rich colors, and dazzling patterns—Yuji's specialty. The essential ingredient of world-renowned Tsugaru lacquer is the sap called *urushi* from the *Rhus verniciflua* tree, a member of the sumac family. It takes about ten to fifteen years for the tree to mature, and after about a cup of sap has been harvested, the tree dies. The sap is then purified and aged for several years.

The beauty of Yuji's work takes time to achieve. To make his project, *The Boat*, Kubo cut beech into thin strips and wound them around a mold. After sealing the beech with a coat of lacquer, he glued cloth to the surface using rice paste and more lacquer. Then he applied a ground of finely crushed clay, raw lacquer, and more rice paste using special spatulas to create a dappled effect. The process requires up to fifty applications of pigmented lacquer, clear lacquer, and other coatings to achieve the hard, smooth, vibrantly colored façade. Unlike normal paint, the lacquer needs a humid atmosphere and several days to dry between coats. Then the lacquer must be laboriously rubbed down to a smooth surface, which reveals the different colors and patterns. The polishing and burnishing process is called *senbenkoguri*, which means, "to polish a thousand times."

b. 1954 Hirosaki, Japan

Background: earned degree in business administration from University of Tokyo, then returned home to work in father's lacquer workshop; Yuji opened his own studio in 1985, specializing in Tsugaru lacquer.

Studio location: Hirosaki, Japan

Four-Drawer Box, 2007. Paulownia, plywood, urushi lacquer; H. 8¼" W. 10" D 5".

Orange Boat, H. 13" W. 18" L. 45". Kubo created this by applying urushi lacquer to the wood. The horns in Kubo's works are created with various woods, including cedar, pine and zelkova, painted with urushi lacquer, and then covered with gold and silver.

Silver Boat, H. 22" W. 18" L. 34". Kubo created this piece by applying charcoal power, silver powder, and urushi lacquer to thin wood. The horns in Kubo's works are created with various woods, including cedar, pine and zelkova, painted with urushi lacquer, and then covered with gold and silver.

The Boat, 2007. Beech, urushi lacquer, gold leaf; H. 7¼" W. 25¼" D. 8¼".
The idea for the shape came from *20,000 Leagues Under the Sea*. The
gold-leafed teeth projecting from the lid recall similar shapes on the
back of the submarine Nautilus; Kubo wants them to suggest speed.

YUJI KUBO

Red and Silver Striped Box, 2008. MDF, urushi lacquer, silver; H. 1¾" W. 3½" D. 3½". Kubo has done a series of square boxes like this, decorated with stripes in different colors.

Sea Shell Box, 2008. Thuja, MDF, sea shell, urushi lacquer, silver; H. 1¾" W. 3½" D. 3½". Seashells embedded in the lacquer and polished flat, suggesting a tile floor, form the checkerboard pattern in *Sea Shell Box.*

YUJI KUBO

PO SHUN LEONG

Po Shun Leong's first boxes featured smooth, curved surfaces that required time-consuming sanding and finishing. Then he began to cut numerous shapes and forms, creating an infinite variety of parts that he glued onto his increasingly complex boxes. He chooses woods for their colors. His boxes, assembled from many small pieces, draw clear influence from the Constructivists including Kazimir Malevich, Wassily Kandinsky, Aleksandr Archipenko, and Naum Gabo. As his boxes got bigger and bigger, he started to make full-size desks, chairs, consoles, and coffee tables using the same technique. Some of his more unusual work takes the form of abstract figures. *Figure,* for example, was inspired by the playful sculpture of the German Surrealist Max Ernst.

b. 1941 Northampton, England

Background: Had formative experience as boy playing with a carved ocean liner while living with a family in the country to escape WWII bombing; earned degree in architecture from Architectural Association School of Architecture, London; went to Mexico with American Friends Service Committee and stayed for 16 years; moved to California in 1981, where he continues to make chairs and boxes.

Studio location: Winnetka, California

www.poshunleong.com

Landscape Box, 2008. Pink ivory, various other woods; H. 24" W. 20" D. 10". The rare pink ivory wood sets off the front of the multi-drawer box.

Metropolis, 2006. Mainly mahogany, maple, ebony; H. 73" W. 31" D. 19". *Metropolis*, an assemblage of tall containers with many drawers and internal lighting, evokes the work of Naum Gabo.

Figure, 2002. Honduran mahogany; H. 60". A visit to an exhibition of the playful sculptures by the early twentieth century German artist, Max Ernst, inspired this piece. The faces in the head rotate to change the expression. She nurtures the golden egg in her belly.

Landscape Box, 2008. Pink ivory, various other woods; H. 24" W. 20" D. 10". The rare pink ivory wood sets off the front of the multi-drawer box.

Ancient City, 2006. Many woods; H. 15" W. 15" D. 10".
Originally a boat-like structure that was drastically
deconstructed. It was again modified for the 2006 Furniture
Society Exhibition called Show Me Your Drawers.

Desk, 1996. Cherry burl; H. 84" W. 48" D. 15". Leong became famous for his boxes and decided to scale them up into full-size furniture. Centered in the desk is a white city rising into a landscape of columns, pyramids, and hills. A golden orb, symbol of harmony and power, sits in the crest.

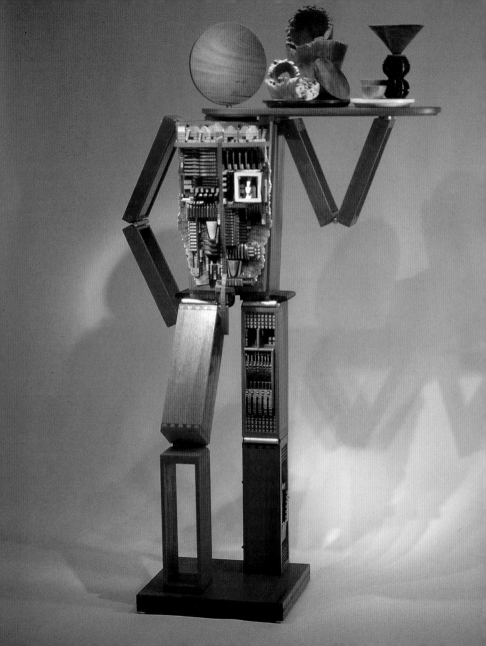

Waiter, 2002. Mainly mahogany; H. 72" W. 48" D. 15". *The Waiter*, who is the same height as woodturner Bob Stocksdale, is holding scrap turnings from his friend's workshop. A wine compartment is concealed in the figure's chest. Made for the Furniture Society's 2003 Cabinets of Curiosities exhibition.

Crescent Box, 1983. Hawaiian Koa; H. 9" W. 12" D. 7".

PETER LLOYD

In his boxes, Peter Lloyd likes the wood—he only uses native British woods—to be the center of attention. Painting or any other eye-grabbing surface treatment he leaves to other artists. While his boxes appear to be straightforward, his prominent wooden hinges and the highly figured wood provide the interest. In addition, he makes everything himself, including the hinges, which often pivot on dowels that project from the box. It's his style.

Beginning a box, he lets the rough board suggest the design. All of his boxes are sanded to a smooth, glassy finish and coated with Danish oil and wax to achieve an inviting tactile surface.

b. 1952 London, England

Background: father was architect; after working as air traffic controller at Heathrow, a woodworking teacher in Botswana, and woodworking teacher in England, Peter went into business for himself in 1990, opening a studio in Cumbria, England, where he has been since.

Studio location: Hallbankgate, England

www.finehardwoodboxes.com

Moue, Box No. 1147, 2008.
Yew, black walnut, velvet;
H. 5" W. 13" D. 8".

Twins, 2007. Bog oak, ripple sycamore; H. 17" W. 15" D. 9".
Lloyd calls *Twins* his skeleton box. The idea came from the
inside out. He started with the trays, decided they could
be drawers, and got to thinking about the bare minimum
of material needed to support them.

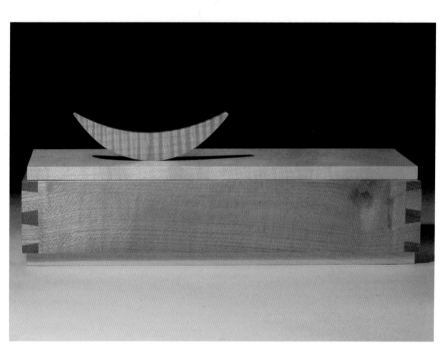

Crescent Box, 2008. Elm,
Sycamore; H. 3" W. 10" D. 4".

PETER LLOYD

Antidote to Computers, 2007. Burl oak; H. 3½" W. 12" D. 7". Lloyd made this for his son's graduation from the university with a degree in multimedia computing. It took a while to find a piece of wood with a natural opening for the circuit board.

Jewelry Box, 2008. Burl oak, ripple sycamore; H. 4" W. 12" D. 7½". Lloyd particularly likes the contrast between the precisely made dovetail joints on the sycamore trays and the raw-edged burl oak.

TOM LOESER

Tom Loeser has spent a great deal of time researching traditional furniture so he can, as he says, "turn the historical furniture inside out or upside down or backward." Sometimes, his material is not traditional, as with his boxes he constructed out of paper and cardboard. The cardboard produced a grain pattern like wood, only coarser, and he carefully cut dovetails to join the boxes as sort of a visual pun.

A pioneer in the realm of painting wood art, Tom studied the work of color theorist Joseph Albers; he is particularly interested in the way adjacent colors interact when painted on wooden surfaces.

b. 1956 Boston, Massachusetts

Background: Worked in ceramics shop for a year before going to college; earned BA in sociology and anthropology from Haverford College, BFA from in furniture design from Boston University, and MFA from University of Massachusetts; worked nine years at Emily Street Cooperative in Boston; has taught at University of Wisconsin, Madison, since 1991.

Studio location: Madison, Wisconsin

www.tomloeser.com

Multiple Complications, 1995. Wood and paint; H. 50" W. 34" D. 21". Multiple Complications seems like a generic chest, but the inside spaces get complicated with drawers inside of drawers inside of drawers. To find the extra drawer requires exploration.

Dovetail Box, 1990. Corrugated paper; H. 15" W. 23" D. 14". Corrugated paper is a completely non-precious material. Loeser achieved various surface effects by cutting the material at different angles. The color comes from sheets of colored paper.

Chest of Drawers, 1989. Mahogany, poplar, Baltic birch, mahogany plywood; H. 73" W. 29" D. 24". Part of the Museum of Fine Arts Boston New American Furniture show, this piece was based on an eighteenth century chest-on-chest Loeser saw in the collection. He deconstructed it and added a painted and carved surface.

TOM LOESER

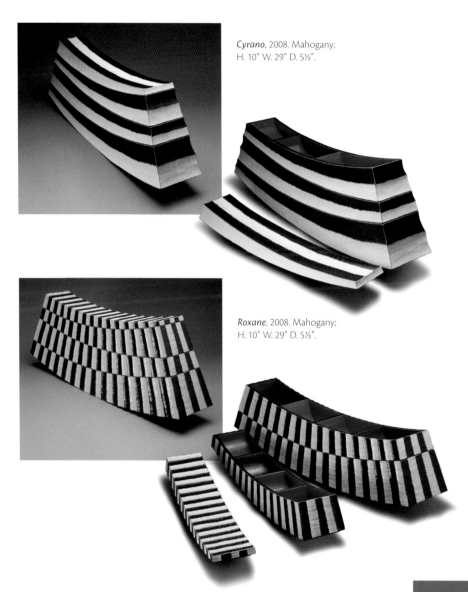

Cyrano, 2008. Mahogany;
H. 10" W. 29" D. 5½".

Roxane, 2008. Mahogany;
H. 10" W. 29" D. 5½".

MICHAEL MODE

In 1992, a decade into his woodturning career, Michael Mode experienced an "A-ha!" moment that would lead to the happy discovery of his signature style. He found himself turning vessels that had lids with wings, curved tips undulating like the fins of a ray, or like the ends of a flying carpet. Then he added graceful domes. It wasn't until flipping through a book on the subject that he realized what he was making recalled the architecture of Mughal India—the empire ruled by Akbar (1556–1605), the inspiration for many of Michael's pieces. Mughal (Persian for "Mongol") architecture pulled together imported Islamic and native Hindu tendencies for an exotic look—the Taj Mahal being the most famous example. Clearly, his two years of travel through the Middle East and residence in Kashmir had made an impression.

Michael turns laminated bowls as well. His method involves turning a layered and glued blank made of concentric rings cut on an angle. The dramatic patterns he achieves have lead him to devote a lot of his studio time to gluing up the blanks. After sealing the surface with superglue, he applies a French polish.

b. 1946 Quakertown, Pennsylvania

Background: Attended Haverford College to study creative writing but left in junior year; traveled to Morocco and Kashmir in two-year tour, absorbing Islamic and Mughal Indian design influences; after moving back home, taught himself woodturning, on a homemade foot-powered lathe, at age 29, then gained experience working for local cabinetmaker, laminating guitar necks; began exhibiting his own work in galleries in 1982.

Studio location: Bristol, Vermont

michaelmode.com

Walking Cathedrals, 2008. Honduran rosewood, mahogany; Max. H. 10" W. 20" (variable) D. 10". Mode's favorite checkerboard pattern runs through his work.

116

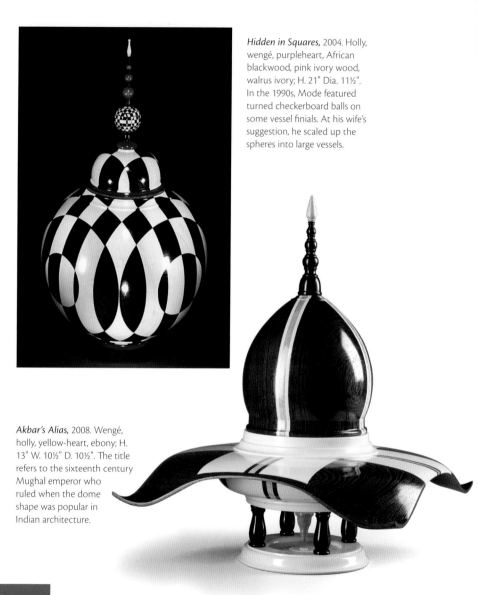

Hidden in Squares, 2004. Holly, wengé, purpleheart, African blackwood, pink ivory wood, walrus ivory; H. 21" Dia. 11½". In the 1990s, Mode featured turned checkerboard balls on some vessel finials. At his wife's suggestion, he scaled up the spheres into large vessels.

Akbar's Alias, 2008. Wengé, holly, yellow-heart, ebony; H. 13" W. 10½" D. 10½". The title refers to the sixteenth century Mughal emperor who ruled when the dome shape was popular in Indian architecture.

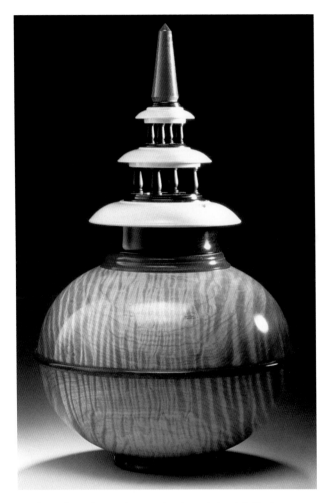

Hollywood Pagoda, 1996. Rosewood, curly maple, jarrah, holly, ebony, pink ivory wood; H. 19" Dia. 12". This is another equator vessel turned in two parts and joined together to suggest an oriental pagoda.

Akbar's Avenue, 2007. Holly, purpleheart, pink ivory wood, ebony, boxwood; H. 12" Dia. 6". Under the lid is a miniature checkerboard and chess set, complete with a pair of tweezers to move the tiny pieces.

Akbar's Affinity, 1998. Holly, ebony, pink ivory wood, purpleheart, wengé; H. 12" W. 19" D. 12". This is one of Mode's favorites in his Winged Vessel series. The piece reflects his interest in Mughal architecture.

CRAIG NUTT

Nutt got the idea for his line of vegetable furniture from his college days, when he organized a marching band whose members dressed up as vegetables and played homemade instruments. As an avid gardener himself, living on a nine-acre farmstead, he uses vegetable shapes and colors to create art with humor and irony. Some of his projects, like Nuclear Medicine Chest, are more overtly satirical, while others, like his tables with cement tops and mahogany trim, speak to the viewer through the clever unusual juxtaposition of materials.

He prefers non-exotic wood, buying pine and poplar from his local lumberyard, or salvaging trees that have been felled by wind. His challenge is to figure out how to turn the raw, bland wood into eye-catching art, to force his audience to see mundane objects in a new light.

b. 1950 Belmond, Iowa

Background: Father and Grandfather were tinkerers with their own workshops; Daniel earned a BA in religious studies from University of Alabama before getting job restoring antiques; passion for the work led to becoming self-employed craftsman in 1977; relocated in 1998 to outside Nashville, where he has maintained his studio since.

Studio location: Kingston Springs, Tennessee

www.craignutt.com

Radish Table, 2004. Oil paint on turned and carved wood; H. 29" W. 24" D. 24". *Radish Table* behaves more like a box. Rather than dropping down, the table leaves drop up to allow access to the interior of the radish.

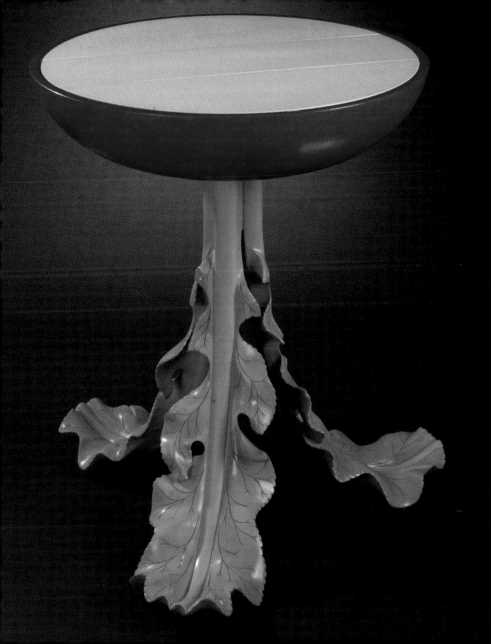

Walnut High-Top, 1985.
Walnut, maple, padauk.

Nuclear Medicine Chest,
1984. Wood, detuned
music box movement; H.
12" W. 5" D. 4½". Inspired
by a cartouche box from
King Tutankhamen's tomb,
Nuclear Medicine Chest
plays "Raindrops Keep
Fallin' on My Head," with
one note out of tune, as
missiles cross the horizon. It
has two drawers for aspirin
and iodine capsules.

Chocolate-Covered Donut Teapot,
2000. Mahogany;
H. 13" W. 16" D. 3¾".

CRAIG NUTT

Donette Teapot, 1999. Mahogany;
H. 9" W. 16" D. 4". This project is
actually a tea caddy designed to
hold a selection of tea bags.

CRAIG NUTT

JAY AND JANET O'ROURKE

In the early 1970s, Jay O'Rourke supported himself by turning flatware, and then by making constructed boxes of all sizes out of exotic woods. Meeting at a craft fair in San Francisco, he and future wife Janet began a partnership that continues today. Their specialty became turned vessels. Janet usually generates the concept, and then Jay constructs the project before turning it back over to Janet, who, as a trained illustrator views carving as a way to draw in three dimensions. Their turned vessels feature highly figured woods in contrasting colors and, often, ornate finials having a natural or mythological theme.

b. 1947 Santa Barbara, California (Jay);
1958 Los Angeles, California (Janet)

Background: Jay grew up watching his father repair motorcycles before repairing surfboards in high school; he subsequently left college to focus on crafts, beginning his career in fine woodworking in 1969. Janet earned her BFA in illustration from Academy of Art College and completed some graduate work at Otis Art Institute of Parsons School of Design.

Studio location: Paducah, Kentucky

jayoboxes.com

Vessel in Bloom, 2008. Spalted Scottish beech, ebony, black pearls, sterling silver; H. 18" Dia. 8".

Pandora's Other Box, 2001.
Purpleheart, ebony, pink ivory, pearls,
gold leaf; H. 12" W. 8" D. 6". The
Pandora is a mermaid holding pearls
and wearing 1940s attire.

Bird in Flight, 2008
Spalted Scottish
beech, ebony,
piassaba palm, Taqua.
Inspired by birds flying
across the Pacific
sunset.

Rabbit Rose, 2008. Cocobolo, ebony, betelnut, palm; H. 18" Dia. 12". Janet always loved rabbits. Rabbits bring good luck.

JAY AND JANET O'ROURKE

Dragonfly, 1999. Pink ivory, Macassar ebony.

JAY AND JANET O'ROURKE

Hinged Boxes, 1971–2008. Smallest: H. ¾" W. 1⅝" D. 1⅜" Largest: H. 1¾" W. 5" D. 4¼". The pieces displayed in *Hinged Boxes* were all Jay's original design. The couple was among the first to sell small, exotic hardwood boxes. The ebony end caps serve as a frame to highlight the highly figured woods.

JAY AND JANET O'ROURKE

EMI OZAWA

A lifelong artist already, Emi Ozawa discovered the concept that would propel her career early on, while studying abroad as an exchange student in Philadelphia in the late 1980s: woodworking as interactive sculpture. She often creates projects using her favorite shape, the circle, which reminds her of completion, mobility, and balance. The circle of a microscopic egg that is the beginning of life is, for her, the original form.

She creates boxes that are meant to act as toys for grown-ups, she says, rather than as utilitarian containers. They usually exhibit kinetic qualities reminiscent of mobiles by Alexander Calder, an artist she admires. In fact she categorizes her container projects as "kinetic sculptures." She wants her containers to provoke viewers' curiosity, especially in the way the lids operate.

b. 1962 Tokyo, Japan

Background: Accountant father and homemaker mother encouraged Emi to take art classes; Emi earned a degree from Joshibi University then, after working in commercial graphic design, enrolled in the Tokyo School of Arts to study sculpture; an exchange program brought her to Philadelphia, where she completed her BFA in 1989; she then earned her MFA in furniture design from the Rhode Island School of Design.

Studio location: Albuquerque, New Mexico

emiozawa.com

Red Bridge, 2008. Maple plywood; H. 20" W. 20" D. 3¼".

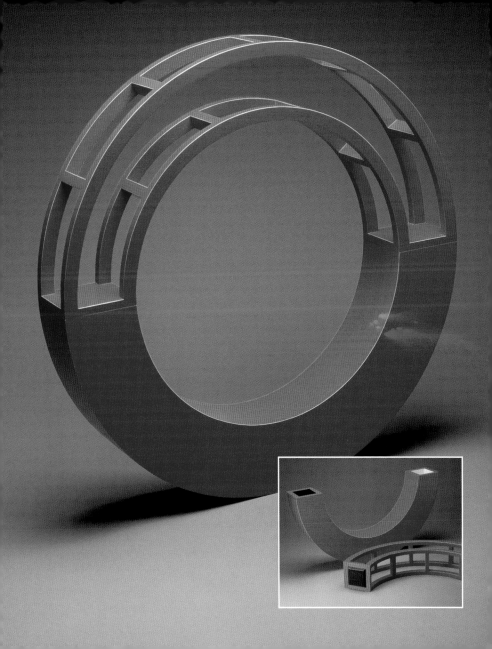

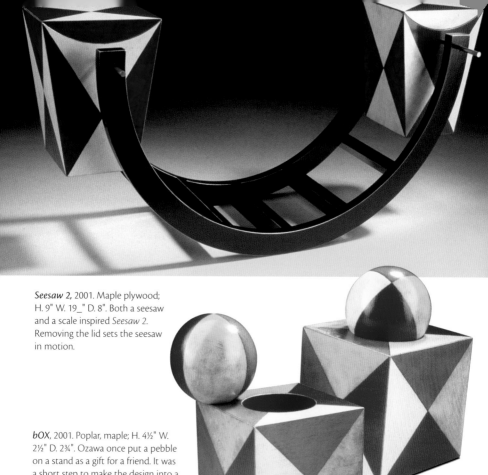

Seesaw 2, 2001. Maple plywood; H. 9" W. 19_" D. 8". Both a seesaw and a scale inspired *Seesaw 2.* Removing the lid sets the seesaw in motion.

bOX, 2001. Poplar, maple; H. 4½" W. 2½" D. 2¾". Ozawa once put a pebble on a stand as a gift for a friend. It was a short step to make the design into a box by drilling a hole in the cube and using a turned ball as a lid. This was the start of her box making.

Cubic Circus, 1996. Mahogany, brass; H. 29" W. 15" D. 10". Ozawa started
to name this piece *Antelope,* but she changed the name to *Cubic Circus*
after the piece was finished when she saw the balancing act between the
lid and the cubes.

Ring Box, 2005. Maple plywood; H. 6¾" W. 6¾" D. 2". *Ring Box* is a continuous hollow tube. When the lid in the upper section of the ring is removed, two openings appear, with the lid acting as a circuit breaker. The shape refers to both a finger ring and a circus ring.

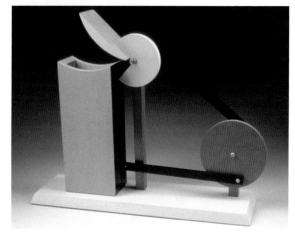

*Quack-Quack,*1999. Maple plywood, cherry; H. 13" W. 17" D. 15". Ozawa remembered an illustration of how Curious George transformed a broom and a ladder into a giraffe, and chairs into leopards and zebras. What began as a pencil box became a duck. The mechanism moves like a locomotive wheel.

Four Quarters, 2001. Cherry, magnet; H. 9" W. 9" D. 3".
Awed by a shining full moon in the midnight sky, Ozawa
made a series of moon-shaped boxes in mahogany. *Four
Quarters* is a painted version.

EMI OZAWA

ANDREW POTOCNIK

As a teacher, Andrew Potocnik has his summers free to travel, which he exploits to the fullest in his quest to study how people around the world use wood in their daily lives. He has a deep appreciation for the material of wood itself; his life's mission is to celebrate wood, which he views as an integral part of man's environment. Through his favorite medium, he conveys the impressions he picks up on his travels, whether they extend only as far as his neighborhood or as far afield as the Nepalese Himalayas, where he's been more than a dozen times.

b. 1963 Melbourne, Australia

Background: Parents were political refugees from Yugoslavia in 1950; Andrew started working with wood early; earned BE in arts and crafts from Melbourne College of Advanced Education; earned ME in Asian studies from Flinders University; works as wood shop teacher while traveling widely during breaks.

Studio location: Melbourne, Australia

www.andrewpotocnik.com

Rosewood Evolution, 2006. Brazilian rosewood; H. 2" W. 11" D. 5". Presenting Potocnik with a piece of rosewood, a magazine editor asked him to make something and write up the process. The photographer brought a fresh eye and created a beautiful image that Potocnik had not seen in it.

ANDREW POTOCNIK

Multi-Axis Box V and *Multi Axis Box VI*, 2008. V: Red gum, gidgee, guitar string; H. 9" Dia. 2⅜". VI: Canthium, western myall, guitar string; H. 8" Dia. 2⅛".

Elm Burl Box, 2006. Elm burl; H. 8" W. 4" D. 3½". One of a series of band-sawn boxes. Using a band saw freed Potocnik to explore new shapes and combinations of materials and color.

ANDREW POTOCNIK

Painted Red Gum Boxes, 2007. Red gum; H 1¾" 3½" D. 3½". Typical of thousands Potocnik has turned as tourist souvenirs, these boxes are made of Australia's iconic red gum and painted to suggest Aboriginal art.

RICHARD RAFFAN

Ceramics have a major influence on Richard Raffan's bowls and cylindrical vessels. He turns his pieces smooth inside and out, sands them with abrasive up to 800 grit, and then finishes his surfaces with linseed oil and beeswax. He avoids high gloss lacquer or varnish because he wants his work to be handled, like pottery. He sometimes ebonizes his boxes with a stain made from rusty nails leeched in vinegar, while he gives others a verdigris finish—he likes to fool people into thinking they are picking up metal boxes. It is all part of his agenda to force people to appreciate his workmanship instead of noticing only the material or the finish.

Similarly, buildings have always inspired his work. His bowls resemble Indian funeral pyres, mosque minarets, and cathedral spires, yet they also recall humbler structures such as African grain stores, European pigeon lofts, or farmers' haystacks. He likes to turn clusters of boxes so they can be rearranged at will, like pieces in a display.

b. 1943 Devon, England

Background: Father was a portrait painter; went to college to study art but dropped out after two years; tried woodturning at the suggestion of his sister, a potter; went into business as woodworker in 1970; emigrated to Australia in 1982; author of numerous books on woodturning.

Studio location: Canberra, Australia

www.richardraffan.com

I don't feel the need to be different, but I would like to be good.

Tower Boxes, 2008. French Boxwood. H. 2" Dia. 1½". Inspired by photographs of Indian burial pyres. H. 4¾" Dia. 1½". H. 4" Dia. 1½". H. 8¾" Dia. 1½". H. 11½" Dia. 1¾".

RICHARD RAFFAN

Citadel Boxes, 2008. Cocobolo; Dia. 3" to 7". For the top to fit snugly to the base, Raffan uses stable seasoned wood for his Citadel Boxes. A Dremel tool cuts the dots around the lid and the base.

Stacks and Pipes, 2005. Oak; H. 14" Dia. 1" to 3". Raffan cuts grooves in his stacks and leaves the pipes smooth.

Box, 2007. Eucalyptus burl; Dia. 6". Like a medieval tower, this box has a lid turned with steps to suggest a roof. Like all of his boxes, these have Raffan's signature suction-fit lids.

RICHARD RAFFAN

Boxes, 2008. Left: Australian dead finish; Dia. 2⅜". Right: Tasmanian horizontal scrub; Dia. 2¹⁵⁄₁₆". Usually box blanks are cut well clear of the pith, but Tasmanian horizontal scrub has solid pith that rarely splits, so boxes can be turned from whole logs that offer striking grain patterns.

ULRIKE SCRIBA

Ulrike Scriba taught herself marquetry techniques through trial and error. Marquetry, a lost art these days, involves designing pictures or, in Ulrike's case, textile-like patterns, to make a veneer illustrated with wood. She does it the old-fashioned way. She stacks thin sheets of different woods, draws a shape on the top sheet, and then cuts the shape into all of the sheets using her scroll saw. She arranges the pieces in an eye-grabbing pattern then glues them to a backing such as plywood. She also makes boxes that involve solid quarter-inch-thick marquetry, with no backing.

To finish her surfaces, she applies Danish oil and polishes using the lathe as a buffer and then adds a final coat of lanolin wax.

In terms of what woods she uses, Ulrike has found that less is more. She prefers bog oak found in gravel pits along her nearby Danube and Main rivers—a good substitute for ebony. She also likes lacewood and European walnut burl.

b. 1944 Worms, Germany

Background: Father was silversmith; studied sculpture at the School of Arts and Crafts in Darmstadt but left after three years to work on restoration of baroque Würzburg Residence in Würzburg; started her own antique restoration business and, in 1976, shifted to marquetry and boxes.

Studio location: Gengenbach, Germany

www.ulrikescriba.com

Untitled Box with Silver Lid, 2004. European walnut, sapeli-pommele, sterling silver; H. 3¾" W. 3⅓" D. 3⅓". Each wood has its own color and figure, but when combined into infinite marquetry patterns, the effect is fresh and intense. The lid shows the embossed pattern that repeats the marquetry on the sides.

Box, 2008. Walnut, ebony, and silver; H. 4⅓" W. 2⅓" D. 2⅓".

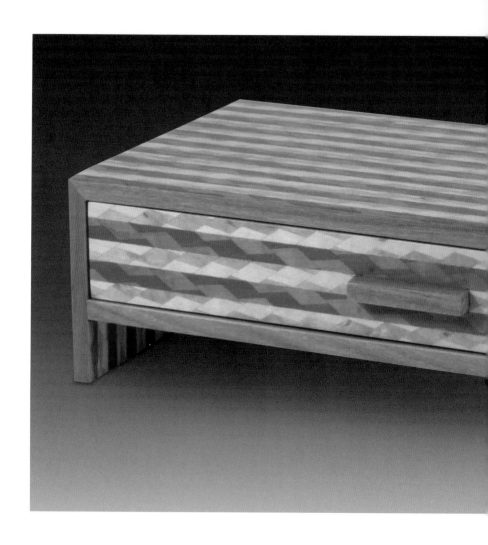

ULRIKE SCRIBA

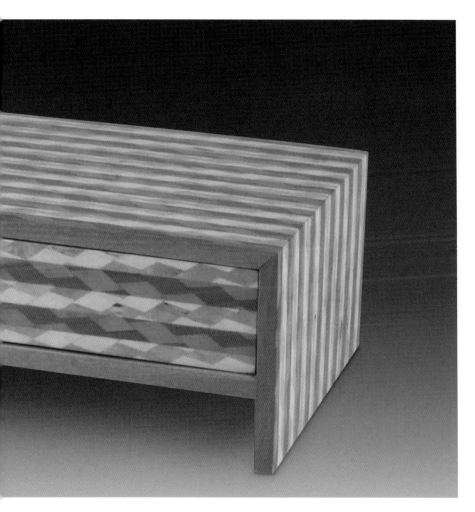

Small Chest of Drawers, 2006. Burl birch, maple, cherry, wild service tree; H. 2¾" W. 10¼" D. 5½". Most of Ulrike's boxes have a lift-off lid, but this box is equipped with a drawer.

Cube Box, 2003. Bubinga, bog oak, koto;
H. 4" W. 4¾" D. 4¾" The decoration suggests
an interesting textile. Scriba cuts a textured
pattern into the bubinga to expose the
marquetry below, like the sgraffito (scratched)
technique in ceramics.

ULRIKE SCRIBA

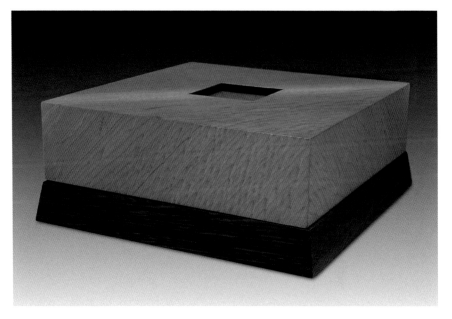

Jewelry Box, 2000. Lebanon Cedar, wengé;
H. 3" W. 17" D. 17". Scriba is best known for
marquetry boxes, but she also has made a few
jewelry boxes out of solid wood. The fragrance
of the cedar and the addition of a secret
compartment add interest.

JEFF AND KATRINA SEATON

Jeff Seaton works within tight parameters. His machinery—an eight-inch jointer, a fifteen-inch surface planer, and a twelve-inch disc sander—places limits on the dimensions of his boxes. Most of his boxes he band saws from blocks of African bubinga, or his favorite wood, cocobolo, a rosewood from Mexico and Central America. For the bottom, he uses a slice of particleboard, which helps make the box stable. He saws the board about a sixteenth of an inch narrower than the width of the box then glues leather on both sides. Once the construction is complete, Katrina helps with finishing and detailing, including adding the patinated copper panels that add interest to more of the couple's recent productions.

b. 1947 Buffalo, New York (Jeff); 1953 Los Angeles, California (Katrina)

Background: Jeff's mother was an artist; he worked construction until turning to fine woodworking in 1973 and specifically boxes, of which he produces hundreds per year. Katrina is a glass artist.

Studio location: Sandia Park, New Mexico

www.seatonwooddesign.com

Some [woods] tell their story visually, others tactilely, or aromatically.

—Jeff Seaton

Mirrored Images, 2008. Australian lacewood, cocobolo, maple, ebony, black palm, Russian masur birch, Cambodian amboyna burl; H. 14" W. 6" D. 6".

Living with Your Flaws, 1989. Hawaiian Koa; H. 5" W. 20" D. 12". Typical of Seaton's early work, *Living with Your Flaws* was cut from a single block of wood with striking figure. As exotic woods have gotten harder to find, Seaton is using more veneers.

Sorrows, 1995. Macassar ebony, copper, black palm; H. 17" W. 7" D. 5". Seaton created *Sorrows* while mourning the loss of a close friend. The figure is a silhouette cut out of copper and laminated onto a piece of ebony.

Flying Fish, 2004. Ebony, cocobolo, maple, Hawaiian koa, satine, copper, silver, gold-plated hardware; H. 15" W. 8" D. 8". *Flying Fish* features Katrina Seaton's copper repoussé work. People frequently note a Japanese influence in the couple's work.

Lacewood Chest, 2007. Australian lacewood,
curly big leaf maple, ebony; H. 6" W. 11" D. 7".
Selecting only the most unusual hardwoods,
the Seatons let the woods tell their story. For
Lacewood Chest, the maple body and the ebony
accents set off the Australian lacewood.

Elliptical Monoliths, Nesting Set, 2006. Cocobolo,
rosewood; H. 15" W. 7" D. 7". The couple's most challenging
design, all three boxes in the set are band sawn out of a
single block of rosewood. Shaker oval boxes and nesting
boxes from Russia inspired the nesting boxes.

TOMMY SIMPSON

Tommy Simpson, the son of a doctor who grew up in the Midwest, followed a winding path to an art career but has been established since the mid-1960s. Early on he made furniture with brightly colored characters and abstract decoration; over time he grew more enamored of his narrative sculptures. He refers to his work as "abstract narratives." His pieces contain historical references and found objects like buttons, brushes, tools, and feathers.

b. 1939 Elgin, Illinois

Background: Attended a number of universities, eventually earning an MFA in painting and printmaking from Cranbrook Academy of Art in 1964; works in a variety of media including jewelry and painting.

Studio location: New Preston, Connecticut

www.tommysimpson.net

Tooling Tennessee Box, 1994. Basswood, iron, and acrylic paint; H. 18" W. 24" D. 10".

The Four Rivers, 2004. Mixed wood; H. 72" W. 32" D. 19". Based on an ancient Persian garden divided into quarters representing the four seasons, the four heavens, and the four winds. Called a "parades," it gave rise to our word paradise.

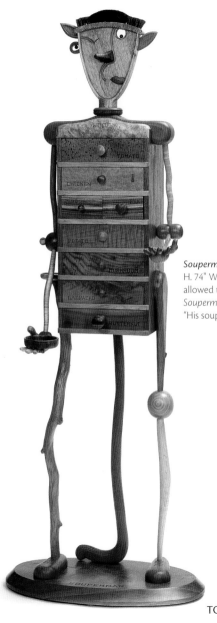

Souperman, 2004. Mixed wood; H. 74" W. 33" D. 18". "I'm not allowed to tell you about the *Souperman,*" whispers Simpson. "His souper-powers are secret."

Night Rambler, 2004. Painted
wood; H. 81" W. 27" D. 15".
Simpson painted the cabinet
of white, varnished it, and
then applied a mixture of
glazes with black pigment
that he scratched through to
reveal the white undercoat.
The effect is much like
children's finger painting.

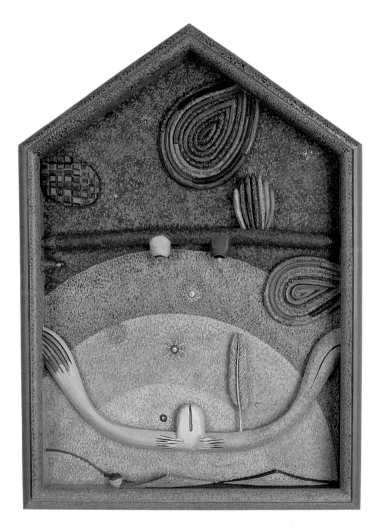

House of Midnight Wants, 1998. Painted wood; H. 27" W. 19½" D. 2¼".
Simpson explains *House of Midnight Wants*: "Our desires take on different
shades of blue, especially when the sun does its evening retreat."

BONNIE KLEIN AND JACQUES VESERY

Before handing them over to her friend and collaborator Jacques Vesery for his carving and painting touches, Bonnie Klein turns her signature spin-top boxes to her precise standards. With long handles and pointed feet, her boxes can be spun like tops, by twisting the handle between thumb and finger and releasing them.

In the late 1990s, Jacques came to the realization that focusing on featuring beautiful wood was not his forte. Instead, he found his unique style of coloring and texturing the surfaces of his projects, and national recognition soon followed. He roughs out his design with a rotary tool and then carves the fine details with a heated knife that he can control with precision. Then he paints the scorched surface with India ink, applying up to seven thin coats in different shades to enhance the texture. For his color decisions, he takes inspiration from the Impressionist painters, who believed that forms were more effectively expressed by color than by line.

b. 1942 Los Angeles, CA (Bonnie); 1960 Westwood, NJ (Jacques)

Background: Bonnie's father was a builder; she attended the University of Hawaii and, in the early 1980s, began her career in woodturning, at first to build her daughter a dollhouse, while also developing and marketing her own line of lathe tools to fill a gap in the market. The son of a machinist; Jacques served in the Navy for four years aboard submarines; in 1987 he began his woodturning career after being gifted a vintage lathe, and in the 1990s began working from his home studio in Maine, where he has maintained his shop since.

Studio location: Renton, Washington (Bonnie); Damariscotta, Maine (Jacques)

www.jacquesvesery.com

As the World Turns & the Seasons Spin, 2009. Swiss pear, white oak, mammoth ivory, silver and gold leaf; H. 6" W. 21" D. 5".

'*Put me in coach, I'm ready to top that,*' 2006. Cherry, holly, maple; H. 6" Dia. 5". Klein turned and Vesery carved and painted '*Put me in coach, I'm ready to top that*' for a baseball exhibit at the Louisville Slugger Museum.

BONNIE KLEIN AND JACQUES VESERY

As the World Turns Green with Envy of the Sun and Moon, 2007. Cherry, pear, koa, glass; H. 6" Dia. 4". Following the 2006 AAW auction, Vesery believed he and Klein could not top the baseball piece, but then on his way home, he sketched this idea for the next auction. It raised record-breaking funds for the AAW education fund.

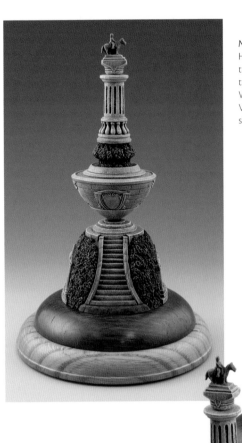

National Treasures, 2008. Historic woods, steel; H. 8" Dia. 5". Vesery and Klein collaborated to make *National Treasures,* an elaborate top, for the annual American Association of Woodturners (AAW) auction in Richmond, Virginia. It uses wood from four historic Virginia sites, including Mount Vernon.

BONNIE KLEIN AND JACQUES VESERY

The Birth of a Fabergé Wanna Be, 2002. Maple, holly, madrone, walnut, gold leaf; H. 7" Dia. 5". Made in collaboration with Klein after an exhibition review said Jacques's work had traits of a Fabergé egg.

PHILIP WEBER

A connoisseur of old black-and-white movies, Philip Weber sees something of that aesthetic reflected in his boxes. He also draws inspiration from the Art Deco movement. When he sets about making a new box, he first settles on a basic shape and size. He trial-fits parts until he likes the result, and then he workshops the prototype at shows, taking orders as a way to gauge enthusiasm for his new designs. This time-tested method generally yields works that have removable lids, even when they recall small sculptural objects, sleek finishes, and sharp lines.

b. 1952 New York, New York

Background: Left college to attend farrier school to make horseshoes, which he left in turn to go into woodworking in 1976, working in a North Carolina furniture factory while developing his own box projects on the side; has been self-employed since 1982 and gained recognition through the 1983 American Craft Council Fair in Rhinebeck, New York.

Studio location: Effort, Pennsylvania

weberboxes.com

Midnight, 2007. Holly, ebony, silver; H. 3" W. 2¼" D. 2¼". As with most of Weber's work, *Midnight* is a study in shapes and their relationships. Two flat sides contrast with the two curved sides, and the handle echoes the curve.

Set Sail, 2007. Holly, leopardwood, ebony; H. 2⅝" W. 6½" D. 3⅜". Although the shape suggests a ship, the title is more metaphorical.

Coco, 2007. Ebony, brass; H. 2⅝" W. 4½" D. 1". Could *Coco* be a take-off on an exotic container by the well-known cosmetic baroness, Coco Chanel? Weber's wife, Klara, thought so and gave it the name.

Primi Tivo, 2006. Ebony, black palm wood, silver; H. 1⅜" W. 1⅞" D. 3¾".
The exposed silver pins could be eyes and the teardrop shape a mouth—
primitive as in Primi, and Tivo as in the modern television recorder.

PHILIP WEBER

Kozma, 2008. Ebony, chakte viga; H. 1⅝" W. 5" D. 2¼". An obvious reference to the early modernist architect, Lajos Kozma, whose work since the fall of the Iron Curtain has gained greater appreciation. Weber saw an exhibition of his work at a museum in Budapest. The lid is glued up from ten strips cut from the same block of wood as the sides.

3-D Deco, 2006. Holly, pink ivory wood, ebony, brass; H. 3⅛" W. 3¾" D. 1¾". As the name implies, Weber is obviously influenced by Art Deco from the 1920s and 1930s. By sanding a brass tube filled with ebony flush to the curved edges, Weber achieves an interesting teardrop shape.

Gateway, 2007. Ebony, chakte viga; H. 4⅝" W. 2⅞" D. 4". This little box conjures up a Japanese temple gate in the mind of the viewer.

Alessi, 2006. Holly, ebony, silver; H. 2⅛" W. 12" D. 3½". Weber made *Alessi* soon after he returned from a visit to Belgium where he saw an exhibit of work by Alessi, the avant-garde Italian housewares company.

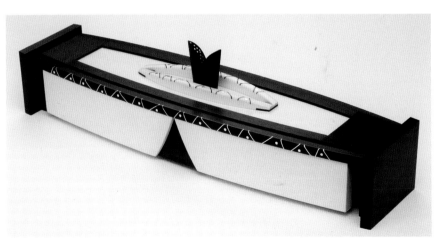

PHILIP WEBER

The Eduardo Series, 2007. Holly, ebony, chakte viga, brass; H. 1⅞" W. 2" D. 2". Boxes in *The Eduardo Series* take on an anthropomorphic look with their square brass eyes and inlaid lines for mouths. Are they the Eduardo brothers?

HANS WEISSFLOG

Hans Weissflog's motto is "Klein und Fein"—"Small and Fine." Coming from a strong design background, Weissflog meticulously plans the fabrication of each piece and sticks to his designs. Nevertheless, about one in three pieces he makes shatters, due to the limitations of the lathe.

His signature Ball Box, with its lattice pattern, is his best-known piece. Often, he makes examples of this design out of two contrasting woods, using the lighter wood, often rare boxwood, for the inside and the darker wood, often African blackwood, for the outside. He also experiments with other geometrical shapes—spheres, ovals, cubes, cones, and pyramids—as well as amorphous forms, like his Drunken Box series, for example. He finishes most of his pieces with two coats of nitrocellulose lacquer.

b. 1954 Hönnersum, Germany

Background: Completed two-year engineering program before becoming technical draftsman for Bosch then Blaupunkt; a layoff led to Hans enrolling in a design program to study furniture and toy design; shifted from making toys and furniture in the 1980s to making boxes and, by the early 1990s, had gained recognition for his sculptures.

Studio location: Hildesheim, Germany

Saturn Box, 1989. Boxwood burl; H. 3" W. 7" D. 5⁵⁄₁₆". Cut from a single piece of boxwood burl.

Saturn for D. Cortes, 1998. Boxwood; H. 1⅜" Dia. 3⅜". After Damaris Cortes criticized his work, Weissflog promised to name a box for the schoolgirl. The ring is loose, but it was all turned from one piece of wood.

Round Square Oval Box, 2000. African blackwood, boxwood; H. 2" W. 2⁵⁄₁₆" D. 2⁵⁄₁₆". Weissflog starts with a sphere, but from the top, the piece looks like a square and from the sides like ovals.

Quarter-Circle Box, 2002. Boxwood, ebony, African blackwood; H. 2⅞" W. 2⅜" D. 2⅜". To get the quarter-circle shape Weissflog puts four pieces of wood together and then turns a whole circle using only two of them.

Ball Boxes, 1996. African blackwood, boxwood; Dia. 2".

Second Drunken Box, 1997. African blackwood; H. 2¹¹⁄₁₆" W. 3⅛" D. 2¹¹⁄₁₆". When *Second Drunken Box* rolls, it travels in two directions, like a "drunken box."

Drunken Box, 1998. Ziricote; H. 2⅝" W. 3⅛" D. 2⅝".
The shape is turned, rotated ninety degrees, and
turned again.

Photo Credits

cover, front flap, iii Tim Barnwell; ii Brad Stanton; iv Andrew Crawford; v Dean Powell; 6–10 courtesy of Oscar P. Fitzgerald; 12–17 courtesy of Bonnie Bishoff and J.M. Syron; 21 Bruce Miller; 22 Scott Finlayson; 30 Archer Photography (top), Stephen Hatcher (bottom); 31 Stephen Sinner; 32 Will Simpson (left), Archer Photography (right); 33 Will Simpson; 34–35 Jean Christophe Couradin; 36–37 Daniel Guilloux; 38–43 Andrew Crawford; 44, 47 Barbara Cullen; 48–55 Mark Johnston; 58 John Carlano; 59–61 Frank Youngs; 62 Louise Hibbert; 68 Imagephotographic; 73 Eyeimagery; 74 Linda Hynson; 75–79 Tim Barnwell; 80, 82–83 Kim Kelzer; 81 Rachel Olsson; 84–89 Steven Kennard; 90–95 Yuji Kubo; 104–109 Peter Lloyd; 111 Bill Frisch; 112–114 Dean Powell; 116–121 Michael Mode; 123, 127 (bottom) John Lucas; 124 Craig Nutt; 126 Bobby Hansson; 128 Caitlin O'Rourke; 130 George Post (left), Bob Barret (right); 132 Hap Sakawa; 133 George Post; 136, 138–139 Mark Johnston; 137 Dean Powell; 146–151 Richard Raffan; 152, 156–157 Ulrike Scriba; 153, 158–159 Paul Clemens; 160 Michael Hamilton; 162 (bottom), 163–165 George Post; 162 (top) Mehosh; 166 Karen LaFleur; 168–171 Brad Stanton; 179–182, 183 (top), 184–185 John Sterling Ruth; 183 (bottom) Dan Kvitka; back cover: Andrew Crawford (top left, top right), Bob Barret (bottom).